Plain Talk Rising

Plain Talk Rising

Mark Dow

PTR

ISBN: 978-0-692-10796-6

Library of Congress Control Number: 2018936884

Published by PTR, New York

ACKNOWLEDGMENTS

My sincere thanks to the editors of magazines in which versions
of these poems have appeared:

Alaska Quarterly Review: "Listener's Guide."
Big City Lit: "Between the Lines and Above the Gaze."
Caribbean Review of Books: "Plain Talk Rising."
Chicago Review: "On Reading Keats's Letters to Fanny Brawne."
Downtown Brooklyn: "Partial Inventory."
Fascicle: "Perforated Evening."
Mudlark: "Certain Uncertain December Days" (excerpt) and
    "Partial Inventory."
New Haven Review: "Interim Agreement."
Pequod: "Certain Uncertain December Days" (excerpt), "Mississippi
    Situation," and "One Fell Swoop."
RealPoetik: "Form of What."
Southern Poetry Review: "Double Lull."
Threepenny Review: "With."
Word Riot: "Water and Light."

"Partial Inventory" first appeared in Spanish, translated by Laura
    Wittner, in *Ojo de Pez*.
"Perforated Evening" appeared, with translation into Spanish by
    Wittner, on *selodicononlofaccio.blogspot.com*.

for my parents

CONTENTS

WITH

Beyond her face the white ceiling,
featureless to just-opened eyes.
Every morning (it probably happened once)
she sat on the edge of my bed and,
hand just touching my hair perhaps,
woke me almost without transition,
hers or mine, and silently because
she knew her presence was enough.
All that was beyond her was my seeing
in the moment of readjustment her,
how she looked at me from her distance
with what then seemed the pity of one
who could see in another what
the other had yet to discover or forget.

Retrospectively it is the sphere of what
I have yet to forget or face up to
recurrently rising in the dream's field
of vision, cut off at the field's edges,
by them. Until the field would incline
and the sphere recede, backward into borrowed
light, all there now and indiscernible. Be or
be like the mother reaching through vision
because she knows, or even has learned,
filling distance with light only illuminates
the distance. And aside from the contact,
or before or beneath but not beyond it,
and whatever happens anyway next,
to wake is to consent: to feel with: to the world.

ONE FELL SWOOP

The father whips the child with his belt,
his the child's own belt, to teach him about
being the bearer and not the receiver
because to receive implies interaction
and he is alone in this. He must know this.
From somewhere the mother watches. Maybe that
is the sad part: who is the one she should go to?
The discomfort of the uneven physical hurt
(the right-handed man stood on the boy's left, behind him,
resultant blows tending toward the latter's right side)
is like a small boat banking, sailing him slowly out to sleep
in the stillness of disappearance that disperses beginnings
in a measure almost equal to the deception they come in.

The fullest trees need more room because there is more
and spread to form the forest canopy's uppermost layer.
Denied light, lower vegetation adapts to less light.
Shadows shift without randomness, changing and perfect.
Responsibility has no place here, a fact they each use,
in fact it guides them, talking, around the kitchen table,
where the family is or are most at home, ubiquitous place,
resembling broad daylight in its uncanny capacity
to bring anything to bear, anything that is not or that is,
that is. To remember and forget are not two opposite acts here
but a single silence swallowed so deep into the clamor there is calm.

The story goes nowhere and on forever. For now
say they rise as one above their separate selves,
the woman trying to come, the man trying not to,
the child who wakes to their struggle walking in,

say they rise above the trees that, joined from above,
hide the house that is their home that echoes now
with cries of need joined to denial in a stilted, lilting plea,
as they blindly soar out over the deadpan deep blue sea.

PLAIN TALK RISING

Started out beseeching no idea whom, nevertheless
severed the breath for stutter-ride through suppleness
of *ey, ee, ay, o, yoo*, sometimes the *wye*, so they'd retain
the openness they've risen from, limitations laid like maps across
the vastnesses and how these make a man feel trapped and free.
Projections of the *t*'s of streets and trees, the lamppost *l*'s,
across and flat on wide wide boulevards and seemingly
inland in the outer band of a coastal plain, an hour's
drive to water but well within reach of the flatness
manifest in land at level with the sea, afloat in lush humidity
of water oaks and palms and pines, whatever lay across the land,
our small yards, ballfields, parking lots, feeder roads alongside of and
entrance ramps onto the freeway perimeter locally known as the loop,
it all effortlessly carried us sky, wide floatings overland to sky
which always was already there with us, horizon everywhere,
each thought and every object at its brim and steadied there.
The sea we're all beside insists the longing's strongest up against
the body it cannot escape, where it diminishes to hold the place it fills,
where it belongs. Since everything stretched out as if there was no end
to spaciousness, we came to think that we were free. Between us, we
believed, were rooms of possibility. All that emptiness got into me.

INTERIM AGREEMENT

Here in the early middle memory starts to hold its own.
For years one mind, or so I thought, it part of me, but recently,
that world complete in terms with which we're yet to come to terms,
secession starts, autonomy yet wholly me. The paths of certain
observable entities are of one of two circling each other ever
since they split, split the moment they were born, voices
bodies emanate even though the receiving one can't be found.
But memory delayed, as in put off, the closing of its curve
until it could survive on its own time. Now, owning time,
reverts to what turns out to be as present as it always was.
The past, alight, hovers nearby with open eyes.

MISSISSIPPI SITUATION

Projected up from the grounded Mississippi city
a funnel of light in the night-sky spreads out

on or at a wide flat cumulus base.
In view of that a decision is made, or was.

The hedge and straddle belong just as much as
we do, since uncertainty is the fruit of distance

and fruit is so natural. From one direction
arrives the overripe and unfallen old.

From one direction the new, arbitrary and strange.
Where they meet is where the protagonist stands,

waiting for his or her name to be called,
or for a soundtrack to indicate just what to feel.

How telling, for example, that out here in the country
the Big Dipper pours out the same dark night

spilling paled through the funnel into urban lives off I-10.
One question is why we call an outlook dark

in which so much is so clearly seen.
Another is why we are right.

Confusion thinks it's desire and wants to be destroyed.
But everything said or moved leaves edges,

gates to contrast, adding to the tangle
projected from out to in or in to out

and back. Nothing is symmetrical
but it will all be when it's done.

What I have learned to think of as the inside
asserts a demand unlike anything in the known world.

The Mississippi situation is not vague so much as
piecemeal, like a vivid dream too hastily recalled.

It keeps being pushed farther back in time.
Soon its wake seems independent, as a vapor trail does

of the barely discernible rumble fading, this
so far from that one of its causes other effects

it might be mistaken for thunder
foreshadowing elsewhere rain.

In view of that, the crystallizing tangle mentioned above
is probably an abandoned web that could be shaken loose,

for clarity's sake, sounding only
the faintest tinkle, like glass rain falling,

without disrupting any other system or lifestyle,
and with almost any concentrated effort there's enough of.

CERTAIN UNCERTAIN DECEMBER DAYS

So this is not the poem
the poem of the body though
it spins and may one day
work its gentle way around
to that, to being, that is,
the one which like a negligée
will drop without a care and drape
revealing through its coverage
the world's suggestive curvature.

The stories begin before I get there.
Squat chunky black birds black
in silhouette, swaying in
the bare rn'wd quier of
the bkyd's 4-story tree,
swaying on it in the wind
prevailing E-NE
I do believe. Some ten of them
I do believe. Two let go,
whooshed out of frame
the window was, another dove (long o)
headlong (and short) into the same.
The first two never opened wings
unless I'm wrong, another headed
right into the wind, banked hard
left hundred eighty degrees
and sailed southwest as well.
Then coalescent bkwd scatter of black
from the four sides of the windowframe
of more than I could think to count

converge as if magnetically like fall reversed,
the tree more bare now now it's been redressed.

A long surrender, then a trembling,
until unforeseeable reassembling.

So lay your burden down and veer.
It's not so much evasion as
a sliding-off-of guided by
unsteadied will or won't.
There's insufficient English here
for this delivery to curve
back toward the straightaway.
The flight trajectory is curved
because the earth is curved, the eye
is curved, the flat TV screen of fidelity
is curved, the metaphors that sort it out
are curved, so projections must account
for English's natural distortions
and the self-fulfilling swell of the space-time, um, continuum.
Note the rhythmic valleys and peaks flattening toward uniformity
in the blurred precisions of outer reaches where there's more to come.

Oh and another thing.
The body of the poem of the body
no matter its shape
will not or cannot keep taking
leave of itself to wander.
Wander it will but it will cohere,
will take but take on

in, and in distilled breath
give back not a part of itself
which is a dismantling
but its whole self, there
by losing nothing, there-
by losing nothing, losses
an integration of echoed shapes,
the shapes of these spaces
in the body of the poem of the body
which this cannot be because
the pencil penning's held too tight,
each space's shape aligning and eliding
with the space's shapes as parts
that constitute some intuited whole
sung almost involuntarily and
with each falling and rising,
with each hidden, inviting breath.
The weight of a body in water
can be measured by the volume
of water it displaces, given
the tools for measurement.
The lyric rises; heavy, man.

Metaphor's more or less
than people think. It is. Is
the groove of deeper congruence
where what fits it's what
one feels one finds there,
or's found to be already felt,
in which an opening opened
what closing became approach.

Small songs unwind. Sky's
oddly orange and the snow
that's wet's becoming rain,
mind's analog sluice
reflected in the way
we tend to see ourselves.
It's always possible to return to
the point at which extension began
to draw the line that goes both ways.
"Thus Descartes was not so far from truth
when he believed he must exclude
the existence of an empty space.
The notion indeed appears absurd
as long as physical reality is seen
exclusively in ponderable bodies,"
Einstein will write. Well, duh.
Omniscience is nothing to fear, but
what of some pain that diminishes
along the spectrum of perceptible tones
to utter silence before the articulation
of it can shape it flush to fit
and hold still in the ongoing body
or room of its resonant dwell?

Although it seems to contradict
the movement of the ways
in which we're moved,
the rising of a lyric wave,
as the force from underneath grows
greater than the shallows can support,
toward crashing then, shouldn't each

move or movement be adequate end?
You know by now that when you look
away is when it all falls into place.
Evolutionarily what you had
most intended and therefore forgot
turns out to be the most fitting,
that will-formed click.
The meaningness
of openness
is
that it
is
is,
first light suffused by cloudiness
so uniform the gray-blue light
soaked through to visibility
seems not to come from any place.
Bare fir's furthermost branchings
or for-now finalmost reachings
just barely sway, as if
what moved them weren't the wind
outside them but some motion in.

The fear of finishing's the same
fear as the fear of setting out,
and fear that feared to fare too far
has steered right clear of this stay here.
And now December's done, oh dear.
One last thing about *of fear*.
The *o* of *of* encircles, but the *f*,
unbalanced, reaches through.

They sound like one *f*, but it's two.
Don't make too much of that, or do,
prepositions rotating pulleys
the rigging links or linking rigs
yield to to restrain the masts and spans.
And tired *i* rests its tiny case,
floats stalk to sky, a buoy
at horizon ledge, a point
in search of line or gravitating
toward some outmost globe or
just afloat. The body,
knowing something's up,
can't put its finger on it though
it's right on the tip of its tongue,
so lies down like some underling
underlining the weight of what it's
like to surrender one's will so
as to emphasize what rides right
above and finds its precise height
matters more now now it's laid out.
What light does is not fall but has
gotten or been gotten down here
to wake me up from heavy sleep
above this murmuring in incomplete
circles all night beneath the flat bed.
It's all the same to me and gone
before I get there to get to glimpse
mine own eyes in the mirror close,
z-sound, to see them to close,
mind's sleep-shudder shuttered
against blue day of sky.

Say that again, against,
the very being here belonging and
estrangement both, how that can be,
that that's just what being is,
the boundary and the being in,
white walls white-blue again
with promissory angularities,
wind as usual invisible
through the window framing it,
making certain the boundaries
and that the body knows just where
they are or where they start at, where
the outside side most certainly begins.

A POEM BY MARK DOW

                                    might have started just
like that with some easygoing banter before
unfolding to take itself too seriously for nothing
at all, least of all in the mind of its repetitive maker
seemingly leaving to re-start what was already done.

Before he's lost or bored you through the door you're
headed for and Mark Dow looped around to head
you off at so that he could open it in time if he can
find the handle, he'll try to make up for the fact
he's always been unable to make things up

and turns, in fact, to find my breath leads back to
back to him and then the outside's renewed as if
windows had been washed in Mark Dow's absence.
His poems are nothing but I enjoy saying them to
you or reading them to myself to see if I'm here.

Believe you me, he wants to return to the places
the images come from I've kept inside him too long.
There's this one recurring asphalt lot where stripes
marked down for parking ride the buckled waves
cracks meander and woody burrs and fleeting thoughts

glide up on through as if accident and its opposite were
one goddamned thing. Guy I know goes it's like
a whisper you can't quite place turns out to be
involutions in the corner of some empty warehouse
elaborating as they aspire to their own proud demise.

TO THE WRITER

Just pause, my pencil. Don't erase
these lines because they come to mind
haphazardly or unaligned.
In time they may fall into place.

CLARIFICATION

Abstraction is a drawing-from.
The distillate rains one down.

PERFORATED EVENING

Drops splat onto the warm and wet cement,
patter the teeming tin gutter along the jutted rooftop,
tick scattered tocks there and whisper dots to puddles
sporadically as piss trickling from an old man's dick.
Electric strokes zag through the zillion tiny holes.
Rivulets meander windshield toward extensive blue hood, eventually sea.
Cracked black seal along the windshield might just need to be replaced.

DOUBLE LULL

Middle-night rain with two voices, one through the window to the left on the street where the traffic lights click, the other out the right one opening to the porch that's open to the walkway perpendicular to the street. Enter from the side. Pass by a palm frond fallen and dried and re-wetted to rotting with days of rain pooled in the crownshaft that wrapped the frond to the trunk's slender neck. In the pool in the crownshaft fifty-some-odd hard candies with tiny tongues attached are snails. Mouth is filled with teeth the tongue touches. The way back from's the way through, and the pull that makes it a rocking despite that hard word is something soft. Each drop separately plops. The whispered chorus is hushing and cool, words blurred to pure sound, assured sound back on shore.

PARTIAL INVENTORY OF IMMEDIATE SURROUNDINGS
OMITTED FROM THE PRECEDING POEM

Cans of Sterno, the Virgin,
a cracked, uncoiled garden hose,
unplugged electronic cash register,
a palette of ten-speed bikes,
dusty back issues of *Elle*.
A power saw without a blade.
Stacks of plywood, coils of blue
nylon rope, unopened underwear,
number-ten cans of curry paste
and pickled Indonesian beets.
Wall calendar from last year
with photographs of national parks,
six or seven toilet seats, a sombrero.
Cigar boxes covered with glitter and glue.
A Wiffle ball, sunglasses,
the Los Angeles County
Driver's Education Handbook,
mouse droppings, mouse traps,
signed pictures of ex-presidents,
pinball machine, crucifix,
small bronze Buddha,
and about a thousand cheap spoons
of every conceivable size.

BETWEEN THE LINES AND ABOVE THE GAZE, WHICH IS A PHRASE OF MALLARMÉ'S

After all, in the beginning were creation
riffs one told oneself one overheard yet
felt oneself to be the primary recipient of.
An unseen but reliably calculated fabric is strung
along to cover the heart, snug and sung, shadows
more substantial than the trees, fence slats,
and polygonal aluminum lamppost casings
they're cast by, through, or with the necessary
help of, across a flagstone walkway which ends
at a chain-link fence spring's first, to this eye,
butterfly zitters back or forth through as
if it were nothing. Its ungainly signature
bears some relation to colors we can't even
see; how odd; though we can see others.
It may be that you're the window and the
being seen through it at once and between.
What's most invisible's the main thing, after all.

One man's surface is out of another man's depth.
I say this because the two can be confused
and because I like the way that it sounds.
Fisherman flings and weights pull the mesh
farther into its form as it morphs with wavelets
pier-lamps catch the crisp edges of and sinks
above a bottom-feeding shadow only the quiet
expert saw, a ray-shaped liquefaction, one or
two hundred four- and five-inch shallow-water
sardines which in an hour'll be floured and fried.
The bubble of z's rises, is squeezed against
the ceiling of my finite conceivings and endless

misconceptions, leaving its elastic boundary
in the shape of the rectilinear frame until
the sleeper gets jambed between sheetrock
and doze. You knows how one's architecture's
disposed, echoes and conforms to what's inside
and outside it. My living room unconsciously
reduplicates the street, the clouds adapt
my headcrown curls and are on their way,
alarm clock buzz a soothing electric hum.
Even what's seemingly self-contained
can wheeze down into a lapse if someone
trips across Ariadne's cord. The knotted
thread via which I had hoped to escape is cut
by the distraction of the sight of a girl's
trampoline takeoff through the trees. She's
in the next backyard. From this side of the front
windows the planes climbing through takeoffs
fly toward me, from this side of the back
away. Everything can be oriented around
anything else. I fail again in failing
to cease being the center the world and all
revolves upon, around, so wedge a lever
and on three. There's got to be a way to
get this thing down if someone got it up.
Go on and aim your own divining rod
at like delights, delights the likes of which
you'd like to turn the dark on in, seize
the slippery eye of her intuition whose
salty melting creamsicle no ice cream truck
can hold a candle to. Polar opposites spot
one another from a long ways off and

in the closing-down distance as distant or
close as long-lost-to-each-other relations,
identical twins bearing not the slightest
resemblance except that each one's essence,
which eats you, lines the edges of its other's
inexhaustible shape. Thus those moments or
months are hours or years when the knowing
and the not-knowing, foam and shallow clarities,
slip from foot-bottom and between your toes,
rug out from under, one tongue of something
else that is not you or else is and loves you like
itself, or doesn't know your name, or both.

As always I'd been picturing the liquid
juncture where what's slipping away is one
basis on which what's coming in over it rides.
We're usually most oblivious to what we most
depend upon. I know you know. That's what
we do. Repeat. I know you know. Do what
we do. Repeat and rise each day and so on.
I had been picturing watery tongues in
the special mouths and the expanding
silence of sorts between arrival and departure,
just picturing them inside of my mind is all.
Not so lonely here as it seems, only more so.
Mike is the grillman, Lillian's looking to get
laid, Alma is quiet but not quite shy, Bob's
a former Deputy Assistant Attorney General,
Selene a social worker with a no-nonsense heart
and small teeth, Deb will surprise you with a joke
just as she goes, George is willing to be amused

but stays out of the picture, Patrick conceals
great anger, Arieanne dances with careful abandon,
Elvin is friendly as well as flamboyant, Beth
is not ill-at-ease when there's not much to say,
slender Barbara's ardent tenderness has
hardened with her having something to prove,
Anna is rejuvenated on meeting someone
from her hometown, and they switch to their
native tongue to converse while Ron
willingly waits, seems to know exactly
who he is, Jeff less so, like Elizabeth, who
is searching but not sure she is doing so,
and the other Elizabeth turns sidewise, laughs
softly and hard, straightforward in her under-
stated beauty; as you can see, she has fallen
for me. I'll see some of them never again,
be some of them always. It's been a crowded
week-to-ten-days, the world revolves around
each one, and here they are adjoining, threaded
through the DJ's persuasive segues even if they
lack some deeper naturalness as of some river's
meanderings, a doodling persistence which when
seen from above seems to return where it sees fit.

One I now leaves me out of this, confident
that as a approaches z off-stage, round back,
in character as ever, that the map of it all
based on a one-to-one scale of it all will
completely unfold as it falls like some blanket
one will finish refolding while the other one drives.
Speaking of ignition, Gide observes that the gap

between opposing tendencies that pull you apart
but which you hold together by not being able
to let go, produces the spark that drives you.
Avoid corrosion, gauge the gap, nourish the spark.
To know what someone is trying to say who
hasn't said it, or, because you know it, has, is it.
Funny how the puzzle seems most disjointed
with all the pieces spread out in front of one.
Does everyone fight something without form,
something formless, I mean, something parsed
to powder mistaken for nothing while meanwhile
slipped above the radar and re-forming itself on
a wider perimeter, formlessness notwithstanding,
the destroyer at its center regenerating waves,
or is that just me? There are signs of hope
everywhere, though, though they seem,
I seem to say, to require a certain degree
of interpretation. Yes, my reach may well
be almost arbitrary, no, I am not feeling one
hundred percent. One of the dancers suggests
my idea of imagination presupposes a gap
between itself and the act; you should have seen
how she rested her fingertips on the fine skin
the cut in her sky-blue v-neck sweater revealed.

Rain drips that almost stopped dropping
adhere to a woody vine and except for
transparency are indistinguishable
from the nodes wherein buds nod thinking through
the ramifications of making their first move, but
enough about me. It's a fat wet spring. In fact

I just got wet when you said that. The rain in slanty
elongations is a just-this-side-of-visible scrim
rushing down through its own faint applause
into a shallow dip on a tarred rooftop that looked
level until rainwater filled it. In the roundish
puddle ringlets ripple scattershot, and in
the impromptu gutter tributary one motion
reconsiders the street's slightly sloped spread,
gist horizontal, while drops re-supply the reservoir
as if materialized inches above before impact,
soft circles of landing despite the gravity's
louder intentions, a kind of cognitive dissonance
which our wider awareness of water will one
day wear away. Uniformity opens the doors
to subtler gradations. Here's all I've been
wanting for some time now to tell.
Rising through takeoff, a silver stylus slits
the blue bowl, bowing its tight trail straight
above the crisp-edged daylight moon one might
say's brighter than the sun since one can see it.
As the vapor begins its visible dispersal,
its chalky bleed into the sapphire sparkling
all the more when flaked against the grain,
as the vapor trail starts widening, i.e.,
coming apart, it also floats, or should I say
sinks, downward, in front of the afternoon moon.
The tiny blade or plane, more sharply lit by
the same sun, is farther west but still in sight,
drifting as if of its own accord, just ahead
of its tail, and silently centered in the mouth
of a muffled, rolling roar that detaches itself

and exhales further, underlines the flat face,
becomes an alto-cirrus at about 10,000 feet.
Another departure already exhausts a fresh
brushstroke more or less where the previous
one just was.
                    Children make up the rules
and mean it and change them as they go. It's
because they don't stand out from themselves
the way we do. In other words it's just because.
In other words, as one ant reacting to
the trail is like one neuron, and, when we
zoom out to the bridge the colony makes
of itself so that it, the colony, can cross
a gap by crossing over itself across it,
part of a brain, ghost of which is
a mind, a kind of spirit that senses
the scent as it exudes it, following,
which is obedience, following itself,
which is freedom, even if encircled, so
I see the lower leaves of the elm melt
in the twilight's steady orange nonchalance,
beside it a woman's bouffant holds gold,
down the sidestreet the sunset sets, dots
as it dissolves, seeps through the world as
we know it, everything bathing as the leaves
were bathed, the light being still, being
what is shimmering, cemented over brickwork
bathing, dogs half-asleep on the sidewalks
bathing, the gazes across the grass unfolding,
traffic swimming, glassy ambers glorified
along with us in the freshening dusk-wash.

I don't know who's who and find no quieted
place to surrender, had only been
trying to say that one day I lay down
and saw the moon, bright in the afternoon,
and that a plane left a vapor trail above it
which crossed in front of it as it dissolved
and as another was drawn where it had been.
So what is that dusk-orange that drops down
to particulate gold and is suffused and upholds
and envelops not just us and these trees but all
networks of reaching and some unforeseen embrace,
a melancholy rendezvous with something in the air?
The existence of existence is almost too much
to bear, yet as it approaches dissolution falls
lightly on the recently coalesced stepping-
stones in the waters we can't help but keep
missing in the sense of knowing they're there
while denying ourselves the surrender to say so.
I'm surprised to hear myself say so, but one can
feel the arrival coming in more ways than one.
What one of the rabbis essentially said is
free will is determined. Healthy organisms
know what is outside themselves, which is what
is not themselves. Therefore, what is outside is
inside, at least in its opener more negative form.
Blink and return. I'm repeating myself.
Living systems regulate themselves and know
when closing time is. Thanks for coming.
I was born on my birthday, someday later I'll die;
everybody. The loose ends are not, it turns out,

lifelines, so why not let the wind lift them from our
open hands, send them back into continuous flight
from where they might be scattered at our feet. One
last thing. A steely shimmer sees or is seen from
a dreamed-of height; it's unheard of; I should know;
some splendid smooth and gently jagged lullaby
has kept me waking now for nights on end on end.

GAZE: REPRISE

what's most invisible
the window and through it
the way that it sounds

refreshed in clear pause
pooled rushings
waters at the join

farther into form
living room street
headcrown curls

the slippery eye
the edges
the liquid juncture

what's slipping away
what's coming in over
watery tongues picture

what someone who hasn't said it is saying

silver stylus slits blue bowl
spirit senses its scent
elm leaves melt orange

existence of existence closing time

FORM OF WHAT

If trains or trails through woods or cortex
buckle like pavement, disrupting overlapping
underground systems of utilities, or are caused to
break by a breaking or broken conduit beneath them,
or even if they're smooth as silk, fallen to the form
of what, in hiding, they entice to and reveal,
arc or act or idea motionlessly risen
and cascading down then again to the plains,
they're what remain and remind us
which rises we walk on will remain
after we've moved far from where
we can remember if our memory
is truly of what led us here
and then sashayed us gently down.

ON READING KEATS'S LETTERS TO FANNY BRAWNE

The great sea opens its greatness up greatly,
freeing all ourselves freely to respond.
Nowhere but here is there what we see here,
so low and smooth, redundant and ineffective,
timelessly forlorn and justly deserved. Strive for this,
for no higher than all suns rise is descent beginning
wrecklessly to transmit itself, fully if not
thoroughly and with conviction. Such treatment
bespeaks itself: having what there is and wanting it too,
wanting something more, like it, yet keeping it far
away, far, far away. Justly so, so the story goes,
roaring the necessary period of waiting. Spotted blue skies
are speckled with sky-clouds. This is the matter,
the earliest foundation mercilessly exposed, put there by hand.

LISTENER'S GUIDE

So sad and unbearably sad these nocturnes, listen,
beneath the glimmering of hope ballooning
into a march now, puffed-up nationalist fluff
bouncing precariously against a sad sad current beneath,

the current resumes its far truer tale now,
a gentle cascadence flubbles across sentimental's throbs,
the sadder true current buoys that and then resurfaces
insistently whispering its passive meandering unfathomable way.

*

Urgent tickles flutter the dark surface
but windlessly, to a bend of sparely shaded nuance,
nuance of adoring, of forgiveness, of pause and,
unanswered, resuming, and pause and climbs a higher resistance, an acceptance,

an opening flatness of settling, of settling all,
watersky flatupon marshlike meadow now, dark now,
new until, one imagines, first light again comes,
until unbearable forgiveness bears the sadness across and withdraws.

*

Sadly skimming surface then tenderly insistent,
plumbing staggered depths to mourn the irretrievable
what, to revive a continuity, a countenance of calm,
calm true, true calm, pomp dreams reclothed in elegant determination,

strolling now in wistfulness, one careful step at a time,
resurgence and trembling strung together as memory
of a previous hope unrealized, and fades again
farther this time away fading farther this time and this time away.

WATER AND LIGHT

And finally I left you: you had been gone so long away. So long and far away that your dissolving into the sky that is everything would be nothing. Or will be your going away, which will stay. Part and depart, come apart and return. What I'm saying is we had to split up to survive. So did I. So don't go, and goodbye.

We thrived in the airless dark because we'd been taught that. The chosen few, hidden from view, and a master of ceremonies who didn't know what to do. Or knows but the knowledge is hidden, and the laws are handed on down. It's too soon to tell everything or pretend that I know. First listening in the space here between. A clarity of air in the clear space that has opened or is open now that I turn. The past is here, someone's eyes reappear, they are water and light.

There is a circle of light that floats on the water. There is a circle of yellow light and a whiter light around it. The water is a wide dark circle that goes until sky. In the dark cool of water beneath is the light deeper down. It is here and all around, water floating on the light, I have spoken too soon.

*

Now I'll tell you about the old days now. Mama was an empress and Daddy was a three-leggèd meat-hook man, meaning he hung the meat. More than you could eat. But nobody knew, least not until the whole shebang blew. See it went like this see. Handyman he lived in the neighborhood and was sure handy with his manhood. Mama took a liking to the skirt-hiking and handy-spiking. In walked Daddy on the duo one temperamental day and did what he'd been taught to do, slayed number one and fucked number two. Then they sat down to talk the thing out.

He and I and she and I were a perfect mishpack until I was born. He'd wanted a girl and she'd wanted a boy, and word spread quick as greased merc how crestlopped they both were, but I wouldn't take no for a yes. Until the old angel of light came by and cast a dark shadow upon. Mama was asleep on the inside, bent over at the basin, face dripping with the cool clear cousin of the green-gardened gurgle, when her eyes went to the window through which the following she saw.

Wide sky was a storm-greenish grey sky choking out the light-hearted blue. Overlaying them both was a cone of white light, yellowed perhaps in the contrast, the cone's vertex as high as you could look above the horizon without starting to come back toward your own self again, and spreading like a numinous hoopskirt as it reached the ground what must have been a hundred some-odd miles away straight across the green hills and the homes of long-lost friends. When it reached the ground it was a man in a robe like a gown white as whiteness and a face you just want to take in your hands like cool water from the basin to wash with. At least, she said, till he told what he'd come for.

Did she know who she was, the stranger asked, or was come from? Had she asked in her heart for a child to complete? Did the cool water reminisce?

She: "I am you."

He: "Cutting to be done."

The meat-hook man was not so hard-hearted as you may have been taught to believe, and he was quick to understand, and he wanted to be one of them. So they snipped a clipping from his clapper just to show that he was hers. The neighbors notwithstanding their misunderstanding traipsed across the hills with silver trays sighting and uninviting the lighting from the hills they were crossing with silver trays piled high as the changeable sky with blurred intuition, blessings for cuttings, and rattling pourspouts of rainwater tea.

*

My father cut out. Who could blame him? He'd been cut. Cut bad. And mother, bless her swolled-up heart, made weak soup of the scrap and drank it on down. And then as you might guess gave birth to his return. He looked a lot like me, they said, I looked a lot like her. We danced across the rooftops and looked at each other askance. What I'm trying to tell you is where we come from, what we meant to each other, how long it took us to get here. But I'm not the one who knows. The fool moon keeps on with its quiet.

I'll tell you again where I come from and imagine you've been somewhere like it. I mean I'll imagine. Until you appear. Until you are here. They were on their own and I unaccounted for. Quiet or they'll find you. A stranger walking by the unexpected brightness, the curtains like streams of silver since their window is a tray carrying sky. When the leaves change to yellow the sky will still be blue. The stranger is smiling as he looks at the blue window shining silver and yellow as he passes by for the one thousandth time. He wakes and whistles. So some sleepwalker says.

Now I'll tell you the story my father once told.

"I'll tell you a story and then you can sleep. It's a story the stranger told when he came here the day you were born to come back to say you were going away.

"There was a wind and a rumble that morning sounded like rain coming over low hills. Grew into both ears, then was a clatter and whistle, and I opened my eyes imagining smelling coffee, and your mother was still in the bed next to me, and I touched her to wake her. She said 'there's coffee,' then she woke and said 'oh.'

"There was dust in the air outside that made breathing cleaner, it sparkled, like it wasn't dust at all, like it was water inside the air. He was already next to me when I asked him to tell me a story and he did. Took a deep breath and he did.

"'Have you ever heard a man whistle so sharp and so long,' he began, his front teeth hiss-whistling the *s*-sounds, 'that he bored a narrow tunnel through the wax right on through? Me myself, I was, well, I'd been whistled into myself when I was a boy. A handyman, rag-and-bottle-man, came round one day and I gave him some soup from the stove and we sat on the steps without speaking while he ate, making swallowing sounds and smelling like fresh turned dirt. Then he looked at me with his eyes gleaming so bright that when he asked if I knew how to whistle I thought whistle must mean make your eyes shine like that.

"'He walked back in the house with his bowl and set it in the kitchen and stood there while I watched his back through the screen. I thought, well he is inside our house and I don't know his name. Thought I recognized him for a short minute, then he turned back around and I saw he wasn't who I thought I saw, and he came back down the back steps and said "all right then" and stood himself a few feet away from me facing me. He stood looking like a kiss-fish facing me, and his eyes were glistening again like wet teeth, but I wasn't afraid, sure I was. He started to whistle like he was holding his mouth just right to let a long narrow whistle of thread-sound out. Not quite melodies he made but long soothing mournful springtime sounds streaming out of him as if they were pleased to be free and out his body into the crystal-ridged air again, inside him until it was time, and loved him as they left.

"'Then he was whistling into my navel, my pupik, my belly-hole, filled. The glistening soundless whistling was up above the ridge but in my ears and was the water that cooled me, into me, as I stood astride the water rolling into and from me. I could see so from the inside. I was a body inside of my body, cool water in my belly up through and into the back of, out onto, wide-glidening the cheeksmooth across, gulped and gasped and empty again and clear.

"'I wasn't surprised that he was gone and I missed him. Or my thirst didn't feel like lack but a newness where the water would sometimes be lakesmooth, other times rise clean, sing cleansing and in me, out through mouth and nose and asshole and ears and bellyhole and eyes, and in again like breathing, music that didn't know how not to be free.'"

And I slept.

*

Now is when the next part begins, has begun. The past is coming up fast, but the mirror's too high to see easily into. When our story began was the cutting. Let's start with this. A man cut off a small piece of another man. Hung him out to dry. You'd like to know why. They'd made a deal, let's reveal. He gave the piece of himself that mattered the most to show her how little he meant to himself. Strength becomes weakness, day becomes night, and she wanted them both from that angel of light. Let her tell it.

"I wanted them both," she is saying. "I'd always thought the old man was everything to me until that strange angel one fine day occurred.

"Now the lie I told your father was not untrue. I was his butter rhymed with berry-trickled lines flickering in the blue-melt air. Found the flower, cut it, and he cried or bled. One day he'd be a boy and then he'd know how to love me and say:

"'Sometimes there's a sound we never hear again that passes behind us before we can turn, but nothing's lost. Nothing ever is lost. Yellow whistling into the wider blue. Red moaning into maroon. Green glowing somehow in its flatness somewhere inside the all-around sky.'

"And he said it."

*

The line of light, a flight, is imagined as a line it may well not be at all. Or's the I I imagine, image or engine, scar, bridge, blueprint, loop, keyhole and click, little monolith with shadow as angle of attack, the hairline crack. The dotted *i*'s the come-string from one undone world to the idea preceding it, ceiling the roundish crown breaks or seemed, until the changes came through and through and to. Someone knows the same someone is missing. We'll be there to tell them soon.

"No place for you," they told him. "You have no name, and goodbye."

"Step aside. I'm thirsty inside."

Which they couldn't abide.

When the rains began is when they ran. Only later the light. First was the dark, now the waters, and later the light. Came down in buckets saying "splat" and "take that," and they had to make tracks. That was that. First the waters and the dark a moment fell from him like thirst quenched by the cool, the wet weight quietly, and later the light. So he wakes and drinks the cool water. In his belly the darker begins to dissolve.

Now the way is made for b-b-bubbles starting up. The bubbles are small balls of air in the water round as the moon looks and rising. They are air in the water. The water keeps them air as they pass through the water to the other other air. They are bubbles in the water until the wall is gone when it can go, when the air in the water leaves the water where the water meets the other air. They are brother and sister, they are lover, they are one in the same. Soon they scatter when told they are rising, look down for the first time and imagine they can fall. There had been bubbles puckered rising from the mouths and noseholes, from earholes and eyeholes, assholes and bellyholes and wee tiny pee-holes, laugh, fly, and rising. Now for the first time they note their tongues and rub their eyes.

*

Once upon a time I was born from out between her legs, from inside her. First darkness and water and inklings of light. Cracked water and air and light, the close-by memory of dark. Floating, then the uneven ground under sky, cut-cord nub falls, what will grow there, open all-around light and unbreathing. Where is she now? Gone: I am from her. The mirror's too high to see easily into. There is some peace in the telling, there's some loneliness in peace. Like the light that sometimes cuts me sometimes shows me things. Glowing from inside its own self, the blossom petal singing the secret yellow in its white bracts which whisper in the purple-seared air, and they let shatter the flat color, flow where whitewater's slapdash is splashed into a lucence waiting for one to listen because one will or one won't in the patience and unafraid, like flatness and a spreading across the hills in their stillness unrolling. The gurgle will widen until it finds both ears at once, and the color of what's past is the light whistling into, the mirror shining it out to where it is where we can see it again from, because we said so. The colors are blurring in the wide water that talks and sings. Once we would have said fleeing, but it is only moving across what it's of, a flower of waterflow emerging clear time.

*

"Hush now, I'm talking now. The overheard version was handed on down in a spiral of tell-and-no-telling, so tell this and go.

"'The stranger found his way into each, but not the all, so we all turn from the circle to look for — '

"'Him — '

"'Her.'

"'Yes, and make a new circle — '

"'Around her — '

"'Yes, him.'

"'Until the start is forgotten and — '

"'The heart indemnified.'

"'Which is why it came back.'

"'Or we did.'

"'How did it go?'

"'There were no words.'

"'Wind arrived, the leaves laughed, skies contained themselves, and the child returned and saw but didn't know — '

"'Did so.'

"'Where to turn.'

"'Tell the colors then.'

"'I can't see them.'

"'Who made off with our all?'

"'Not every all, but what mattered.'

"'It's because you didn't trust him.'

"'Or did.'

"'Is he the whistle-man or the one who told one to cut to be whole?'

"'Are they one in the same?'

"'Tell the music.'

"'It's caught — '

"'Like a kite in a tree.'

"'Where's the light?'

"'On the water.'

"'Does that mean it's not free?'"

*

Once upon a time a stranger whispered things just below the threshold of sound and I felt that I loved him. There is a field of water in the wide sky. The water is dark as the sky it is in, no day or night now, but glimmered whispers of light, as if it's the crests and the wrinkles of water alight, the white reflection here and there on the squared water and through opened air. At first the edges of the squared-off field last forever. But forever has changed, he said, and I can see the field floating from here. The scattered whitenesses rise in a breath's effort to circle and rise and are flat again. They are reflections of light from somewhere but no one known knows where. But what do I matter and who told me to tell? That's how they breathe, I said, and brought us here. The words are like that sometimes, like light, like now, reaching too far to forget who they are, sometimes telling the swells that carry them, sometimes talking to themselves, sometimes selflessly sliding down to the flatter spaces that reflect the water-calmed wide-opening sky.

I had a story to tell but the edges were blurred. Instead was a song which your ears might have heard. The hard horizon stops short of the sky and what slipped into that gap was the I, far and up again toward the top-lighted surface that from underneath it here is window to sky, and I can hear myselves about to start starting to sing.

*

The water was dark because the kitchen was dark because the cool air coming in through the wide open window was dark when she walked into the kitchen in the very middle of the night for a drink of cold water in the warm dark in the house where everybody slept fast. A pilot light flew orange and steady and small through the dark to her eyes. They are meeting halfway, the flame-shaped circle steadily wavering, afloat in the air halfway to her, the orange circles burning in the air like a faint itch back behind her eyes.

Then our eyes are adjusting, a pale white bowl beside the sink pouring toward, and a white square of poured-like light there flat on the wood floor. There was light she had not realized, her eyes pulled then as drawn, from the floor up to, through the bowled shape out the wide window into, the pale-light-blued night-sky and up, the bubbles rising up toward the white moon full and small and far away and white-bright and close, up toward what seemed the surface to where the light was coming from to breathe, to reach a surface and breathe there above the sleep or unsleeping, and breathed without gasping as if there was nothing remote or away.

White and a whisper-breeze yellow in the blue, and a bluegreen circle around it. Who is sleeping and who is awake. She breathes through her eyes, her round face bathed, the small faraway moon in through her bellyhole, hard a moment then full and fitting inside her. She feels its weight then, round light inside she feels now inside her, hands down to her belly and rest there, her hands, for a disappeared whisper some familiar stranger's hands, then her hands laid flat on her rounding, her own hands on her, and for the first time he knows she knows he is there. Her and not her, I am her and inside her, am light giving her semblance until I am born. She takes the cool drink of bright light on blue water into, and I am thirsting for air and for water and for light.

אֲ יֹ ן   סֹ וּ ף

אֵ י ן   ס ו ף

looks like it says the end.
It doesn't, though, though
end is in it: it says there is
no end and is one term for
the one considered One,
big O, a.k.a. the creator, as
if there is or were one one.
Considered means taken.
No end means that alone.

STOP ME IF YOU'VE HEARD THIS ONE

CPSIA information can be obtained
at www.ICGtesting.com
Printed in the USA
FFHW022036171118
49452165-53800FF